The Passion of Charles Moore

The Passion of Charles Moore

JEFF HOOD

RESOURCE *Publications* • Eugene, Oregon

THE PASSION OF CHARLES MOORE

Resource Publications
An Imprint of Wipf and Stock Publishers
199 W. 8th Ave., Suite 3
Eugene, OR 97401

www.wipfandstock.com

PAPERBACK ISBN: 978-1-5326-8531-6
HARDCOVER ISBN: 978-1-5326-8532-3
EBOOK ISBN: 978-1-5326-8533-0

Manufactured in the U.S.A.   APRIL 23, 2019

Thich Quang Duc.

Alice Herz.

Norman Morrison.

Roger LaPorte.

Gregory Levey.

Malachi Ritscher.

Charles Moore.

David Buckel.

CONTENTS

1 // BEGINNING

WHAT DOES ONE THINK about the night before they die? Lying in bed, Charles Moore wrestled with the decision he had already made. Charles was desperate for his death to mean something. Tossing and turning, Charles clung to hope that it might. There seemed to be no other way. God was gone. Charles was left to walk this terror alone. The sheets seemed to be the only barrier between his skin and the flames. Just before sunrise, Charles heard a familiar voice. It was time.

Throughout the morning, Charles was tortured by what was to come. The only thing that kept him going was the promise of tomorrow. Saying goodbye to all that he loved, Charles cranked up the engine. The drive was overwhelming. Every intersection was an opportunity to end it all. Charles knew he had to die . . . but he just wanted to be spared the flame. It was too late now. God had already laid out the path. Though none go with him . . . Charles chose to follow. Looking at the gasoline and the matches, Charles knew it wouldn't be long. In the midst of it all, determination was his only solace. Unfortunately, there didn't seem to be enough of it. Charles turned the car off for the last time. In the midst of the familiar spaces, Charles started to utter his final prayers. The agony of it all turned moments into hours. After much time, he was ready.

Reaching into the backseat, Charles picked up the means of execution. Though the gasoline was heavy . . . it was nothing compared to the matches. Those little sticks of fire would end his life. Each one might as well have been a loaded gun. Charles slammed the door shut. This was it.

After some time, Charles changed his mind.

2 // REFLECTIONS

July 3, 2014

Don't You Dare Turn Your Head:
The Self-Immolation of The Rev. Charles Moore

THE FIERY PASSION OF 79-year-old retired United Methodist pastor The Rev. Charles Moore is raging in my soul right now. On June 23 around 5:30pm, Moore exited his vehicle in Grand Saline, Texas, doused his body with gasoline and set himself on fire. After rescue efforts by bystanders, Moore was taken by helicopter to Parkland Hospital in Dallas and eventually died late last night. Based on notes left behind,

Moore chose to self-immolate based on his frustration with the United Methodist Church's position on human sexuality, opposition to the death penalty, disdain for racism (especially in his hometown of Grand Saline) and his deep anger at Southern Methodist University's decision to house the George W. Bush Presidential Center.

Rev. Moore knew how we would react. On June 22, the day before he self-immolated, Moore wrote, "I know that some will judge me insane." When I first shared Moore's story with a table full of people at a Dallas restaurant, everyone immediately declared him insane. I know different.

While a graduate student in history at the University of Alabama, I spent six months studying self-immolations that took place in both the United States and in Vietnam during the Vietnam War. With stark consistency, the persons who self-immolated that I studied were remarkably sane and unquestionably persons of deep conviction. The temptation of the hour will be to turn our heads and call The Rev. Charles Moore insane. If we do . . . we should also turn our heads from Jesus and call him insane too. For we must not forget, Jesus sat in the Garden of Gethsemane and made a conscious clear decision to step out into death . . . just like Moore.

Instead of judging Rev. Moore, maybe we should try to ignite the passion for justice that burned so brightly in his life in ours. When Texas tries to execute Manuel Vasquez on August 6, maybe we should do something more than simply turn our heads and protect our dignity. When our churches and societies ignore racial segregation and discrimination, maybe we should do something more than simply turn our heads and protect our pride. When we are asked to perform a same-sex wedding ceremony or ordain a same-gender loving person, maybe we should do something more than turn our heads and protect our salaries/pensions. When institutional injustices occur all around us, maybe we should do something more that turn our heads and bless them with our silence. I will go to bed this evening thankful for the public witness of The Rev. Charles Moore and pray that the church would garner even an ounce of his passion and courage.

On a personal note, I serve on the Board of Directors of the Texas Coalition to Abolish the Death Penalty. Rev. Moore helped found the organization. Because Moore lived, I am able to do the work that I do. My respect for Moore is unwavering and I am proud to follow in his footsteps. Jesus asks us to give our lives and Moore did.

Tonight my passion for Jesus burns as intensely as ever. When I look straight ahead into the dark, I see Moore's bespectacled image burning. I see Moore giving his life so that others might live. I refuse to turn my head. I know that Jesus is speaking to me from there. The courage of a passionate follower of Jesus can set the world afire with love. May the great martyrdom of The Rev. Charles Moore make it so.

Amen.

July 5, 2014
Journal Entry

The fireworks of Charles Moore continue. What in the hell do they mean? I think they're blowing me up. I'm getting burned. Charles? What do you mean? Come to me once more. I see the flames. I feel the flames. What do I do with them?

July 14, 2014

Across the Borders and Into the Flames: Rev. Charles Moore, Dr. Robert Jeffress, Bishop Yvette Flunder and Us

Resurrection is not possible without death. Rev. Charles Moore knew about resurrection and his fullest revelation of death came about quite violently. The flickering flame at the front of his funeral reminded us of the immolation and alluded to the endless possibilities of resurrection. The world is on fire and Moore wanted us to follow him into the flames.

The death of Rev. Moore is a call to radical discipleship. The problem is that radical discipleship is not taught or even valued in our churches. We want borders and boundaries. We want identities and labels. We want an "us and them" kind of world. There is nothing radical about such normative and violent constructions. We have grown so comfortable with not being like the ones we have othered. The call of Jesus is not "other than them." The call of Jesus is to a love so radically beyond borders that your love engulfs friend and foe alike.

When Dr. Robert Jeffress of First Baptist Dallas claimed Jesus would construct a border fence, I watched person after person trip over each other on Facebook and Twitter to bash the man. Then what? Radical discipleship comes after the bashing (or perhaps after not participating in the bashing in the first place) and is found in the loving that is the doing. Why are we not working to take down all borders? Why do we believe there is anything righteous about living behind a border in the first place? For the follower of Jesus there should be no immigration debate . . . we are called to be a people that refuses to let any border come between us and loving someone else. Daring to try and live beyond borders is a radical step. Loving Dr. Jeffress is divine.

Bishop Yvette Flunder declared in worship today at the Cathedral of Hope, "We serve a both/and kind of God." I am ready for the church to be a both/and kind of church. Fling the doors wide open! Don't let any normative identities or borders get in our way. We must realize that "How do you identify?" or "Where are you from?" are not Gospel questions. God does not care how you identify or where you are from if you can't love your neighbor or your enemies. If you want to follow Jesus . . . then follow him across the borders and into the flames.

Amen.

June 23, 2015
Pushing Into the Flames: Rev. Charles Moore and the Struggle Against Racism

The moisture forming in my eyes caused the screen to grow blurry. The emotion was so heavy that I was having difficulty comprehending the words. On June 23, 2014 around 5:30pm in Grand Saline, Texas, Rev. Charles Moore walked to the front of his car in the middle of a Dollar General parking lot and placed a burning match to his head. Within seconds, Moore's body was engulfed in flames. Despite the efforts of bystanders, Moore died. Upon inspection of the writings he left behind, Moore's family realized that his self-immolation was a protest against racism. Soon after I read the initial article, I called him a martyr and started praying to Moore. In the year since, I haven't stopped. In the midst of difficult struggles for racial justice, I have heard God speak from the bespectacled image of Moore burning over and over.

Not long after I discovered his story, I wrote a piece about Moore's death. Having studied self-immolations in my graduate studies at the University of Alabama, I knew people would try to write him off and call him insane. The problem with such thinking is that it neglects the fact that most self-immolations are highly logical acts of protest. I didn't think Moore was insane then and I don't now. In my piece, I begged people not to turn their heads from Moore's sacrifice. Sadly, I feel like most people did. Within the last year, among a plethora of other offences . . . police brutality has been on the rise, undocumented immigrants are constantly mistreated and brutalized, children of color are brutalized at swimming pools and just last week Mother Emanuel AME Church was shot up by a virulent racist in Charleston, South Carolina. Even in Moore's own United

Methodist Church, people seem to be most comfortable with partial steps that don't speak to the racism and segregation that dominate most church spaces. Over the last year, I have constantly wondered if Moore died in vain.

A few weeks after his death, I attended Moore's funeral. There weren't many people there. Throughout the service, I watched minister after minister try to carefully navigate the events. By following Jesus to death, Moore backed them against the wall. How was any minister supposed to talk about giving your life to Jesus now? My quiet revelation that I admired Moore was met with suspicion and jeers. Regardless of all that was going on, I couldn't take my eyes off of the image of Moore. Out of the excess of his love for God, Moore stepped into the flames. I refused to turn my head.

Months later, I sat alone in a cell at the Dallas County Jail. Earlier, I spoke at a rally against police brutality and helped lead marchers down the streets of Dallas. Now, I was alone. For hours, I just sat there. The demons started whispering. I began to doubt. When I closed my eyes, I saw the burning image and felt the call to simply keep following Jesus. For the remaining hours of my incarceration, I was bolstered by Moore's presence.

From many accounts, Charles Moore was a cantankerous man. While I don't know if our personalities would have meshed in life, I do know that his witness in death has saved my life and activism. I am strengthened in the knowledge that a modern pastor went all the way in the fight against racism. Jesus calls us to give our lives in service to others. I remain impressed that Moore was brave enough to follow the call of God all the way until the end.

Overwhelmed at the assault of a young black girl at a swimming pool in McKinney, Texas last month, I decided to venture out to the spot where Charles Moore self-immolated. I needed a word from God. Driving through the night, I was struck at the desolation of everything. When I pulled into the Dollar General parking lot, I located the exact spot where Moore self-immolated. I saw the burning image of Moore once more. I felt the presence of God in the orange glow. The light of Moore's sacrifice still guides me. I can't look away. I know that there is always more for me to give in the struggle against racism. When I wonder how much will be required, I just close my eyes. In the darkness, I still see the whip of Moore's flames calling me onward.

Amen.

June 27, 2015
Journal Entry

Does it matter whether Charles was a nice guy or not? I'm sure that there were plenty of people who didn't think that Jesus was nice. Like Charles, I'm not concerned with being nice. I'm concerned with following Jesus . . . and if that leads to the flames . . . then, so be it.

June 26, 2016

The Rev. Charles Moore visits me often. For over two years now, I've closed my eyes and felt the pull of his flame. The media attention is over. Too much time has passed for most. Our memories are so frail. I won't ever be able to forget. I still see the flames.

Journal Entry

I held the lighter as tight as I could. Ever since I found it in that infamous Grand Saline parking lot, it has reminded me of the sacrifice of Charles. When I'm trying to make a decision about how far I should go, I pick up the lighter . . . and it's hard to do anything except go all the way. On this anniversary, the lighter is empty . . . all that is left are small sparks. I think about how it only takes a spark to change the world . . . or at least change a few.

Charles' example shouldn't just be about race in Grand Saline. Charles' example belongs to the world. I believe it touches every issue . . . at least, that's what I'm experiencing.

The lighter guides me still.

Instead of judging Rev. Moore, maybe we should try to ignite the passion for justice that burned so brightly in his life in ours. When Texas tries to execute Manuel Vasquez on August 6, maybe we should do something more than simply turn our heads and protect our dignity. When our churches and societies ignore racial segregation and discrimination, maybe we should do something more than simply turn our heads and protect our pride. When we are asked to perform a same-sex wedding ceremony or ordain a same-gender loving person, maybe we should do something more than turn our heads and protect our salaries/pensions. When institutional injustices occur all around us, maybe we should do something more that turn our heads and bless them with our silence. I will go to bed this evening thankful for the public witness of The Rev. Charles Moore and pray that the church would garner even an ounce of his passion and courage.

June 24, 2017

As the lightening crashes on this night, the passion of Rev. Charles Moore visits me again . . .

Journal Entry

Fire seems to obscure the revelation. Then, the flames shoot up. The soul within me begins to warm. As the temperature rises, I don't know how much more that I can take. Then, I see Charles' face. I can't get close enough. I try and try . . . but he is something else now. Through the glasses, his eyes speak to me. I know that he is showing me the way. I know that he wants me to touch the flame. Fear overtakes my soul. Then, it's over.

Will I ever be called to set myself on fire? The question has rattled around in my brain ever since I heard the story. I didn't sleep last night. The flames kept pulling at me. To live is Christ and to die is gain. What if Jesus had been burned at the stake? He would have chosen to go freely. What's the difference between that and Charles? I will lay my life down for my faith. I will give my body for the message of Jesus. I won't stop. I can't stop. Though none go with me, I still will follow.

Charles Moore taught me what it looks like to go all the way . . .

. . . and that's why I call him the St. of Grand Saline.

Tonight my passion for Jesus burns as intensely as ever. When I look straight ahead into the dark, I see Moore's bespectacled image burning. I see Moore giving his life so that others might live. I refuse to turn my head. I know that Jesus is speaking to me from there. The courage of a passionate follower of Jesus can set the world afire with love. May the great martyrdom of The Rev. Charles Moore make it so.

Amen.

April 10, 2018
The Righteous Suicide: On Chosen Sacrifice

I thought about suicide.

Charles Moore revealed this to me.

Darkness fills the room. Light floods my eyes. I am blinded for the moment. I sit up in bed. Is anyone there? Squinting, I see something in the distance. Sight returns. I see a man burning. I hear God. I've never seen such righteousness.

"Kill his ass!" "Let me at him!" "Rip his dick off!" "He won't be teaching that bullshit around here anymore." "Who in the fuck does he think he is?" Fire spewed out of their throats. Sweat dropped from their lips. Rage filled their souls. They grabbed. They kicked. They drug. They bit. The cliff was rapidly approaching. Death was certain. Then, Jesus somehow slipped away. In the midst of it all, the disciples hid to escape death. None of them could believe it when he returned. They were even more shocked when he declared, "My time is not yet here." His time? He was just a dead man. Now, he's declaring that he picks his own time? What manner of man is this?

Suicide is an intentional death at a chosen time by a chosen method. Jesus decided to die when he knew it was time by the method of execution. Such an argument is bolstered by the fact that Jesus didn't choose to die at a chosen time by a chosen method earlier. He could have run. He could have hid. He could have done so many other things than what he did. Jesus chose his intentional death. Jesus committed suicide by proxy. Jesus committed a righteous suicide.

"I have been to the mountaintop . . ." As the crowd cheered, Dr. King sat down and resigned himself to what was ahead. Death was closing in. Dr. King did not hesitate to move forward. When we intentionally move forward with a chosen death, we are committing suicide. When the bullet pierced his body, Dr. King died in the same manner that Jesus did . . . by righteous suicide.

What happens when a suicide is universally condemned? Does the perception of others determine the righteousness of the act? Righteousness seems to deal in motive not perception.

Jim Jones led hundreds and hundreds and hundreds of people to commit suicide or be murdered. Every single one of them were told that they were dying for each other and as a witness to the world. Many, if not most, believed these words to be true and laid down their lives for others. These deaths were righteous deaths . . . righteous suicides. Those pictures of the countless bodies might look different if the viewer considered that many of the dead actually followed the way of Jesus.

The path. The way. The journey. They all lead to the same place. Giving life so that others might have life. Jesus calls us to give our lives . . . our bodies . . . our everything. There is no other way.

Righteous suicide is sometimes the culmination of a life well lived . . . in the pursuit of the call of Jesus. Be careful how you judge. The departed might know Jesus far better than you do.

I arose out of my bed. Within a few steps, I was in the parking lot of a strip mall. I saw him pour the gasoline. I saw him light the flame. I saw him explode. I knew I should be horrified. I wasn't. The light drew me closer and closer and closer. Ultimately, I ended up in the flames. I felt the burn. I felt everything. I felt eternity. There God found me and in God I was found.

Charles Moore revealed this to me.

I thought about suicide.

Amen.

June 23, 2018
Journal Entry

She is dead. There wasn't anything particularly spectacular about her death. She is simply dead. While the flame of Charles Moore burns brightly in my soul, I can't help but be consumed with the darkness of losing my grandmother. I will not write on this anniversary of Charles' self-immolation. I just need to feel his flame. Maybe I can pull something together later.

January 1, 2019
Journal Entry

What would Charles do this year?
    May the flames burn eternally.
    Amen.

3 // LINEAGE

THE IMMOLATION OF CHARLES Moore did not occur in a vacuum. For decades, Charles saw the immolations of others. Every flame seemed to pull him closer to his own moment. By his own admission, Charles' understanding of immolation began with a Buddhist monk named Thich Quang Duc's immolation to protest the many human rights abuses in South Vietnam under President Ngo Dinh Diem's government. In order to understand, you have to go back to those flames and follow their path until they got to Charles.

By 1963, the Roman Catholic President of South Vietnam, President Diem, had removed Buddhists from all positions of influence in society. Catholics controlled everything and brutally oppressed the Buddhist minority. In May, President Diem banned all liturgical celebrations on the birthday of Gautama Buddha. Rage fomented in the souls of the Buddhists and they began to take up their liturgical flags and march on the government. On May 8, a group marched on the national broadcasting station and faced down government troops. With little to no warning, the troops fired. Eight Buddhist bodies were dead on the ground. Despite fierce protests, President Diem refused to apologize and responded with increased force. In the midst of such injustice, Thich Quang Duc lit his flame.

June 11, 1963. For most, it's just another day in history. Then, they see the pictures. After that, nothing is ever the same.

For bystanders, the protest looked like many of the others. Processing from the local pagoda, 350 monks and nuns walked in lockstep to protest the Diem regime. There was only one difference. In the front of the procession, a blue car led the way. The car stopped at the corner of Phan Dinh Phung Boulevard and Le Van Duyet Street. Monks and nuns encircled the car . . . they were all hold signs protesting the Diem regime in both Vietnamese and English. In the midst of it all, nobody seemed to know what was going on. Then, the door swung open and the procession reverently made way for an elderly monk . . . Thich Quang Duc. Bystanders had trouble figuring out what was going on. It didn't take long for everyone to figure it out.

Two younger monks followed Duc to a specific spot. One held a cushion. Bystanders thought that the elderly monk was going to sit down and teach. Then, another young monk followed behind with a can of gasoline. Everybody thought that there had to be a logical explanation for the fuel. There was to be no explanation. There was only the witness of the flames.

With the assistance of the younger monks, Thich Quang Duc sat down and assumed the lotus position. I can't imagine what he was thinking. I just know that he was determined. Responding to some unspoken cue, the younger monk started pouring gasoline on his head. As the liquid rolled down his skin, irritation set in. Some sort of preview I guess. Regardless, there is no way that Duc knew what was coming. How could anybody? For a long time, Duc clutched his beads in prayer. With fierce determination,

Duc recited the homage to Amitabha Buddha, *Nam Mo A Di Da Phat*.

Then he picked up a match. What was he thinking when he was holding that match? In silence, Duc lit the flame and dropped it into his lap. Flames shot up to the sky. Nobody who understood what was going on could turn their head. In time, Duc's head simply falls to his lap. Pictures were disseminated to the entire world. I have never been able to turn away. Charles couldn't either.

Immediately after the flames began to subside, monks and nuns started to hand out the last words of Duc . . . a plea for justice.

> *Before closing my eyes and moving towards the great vision of the Buddha, I respectfully plead to President Ngo Dinh Diem to take a mind of compassion towards the people of this nation and implement religious equality to maintain the eternal strength of our homeland. Furthermore, I call on all venerables, reverends, members of the sangha, and lay Buddhists to organize in solidarity to make sacrifices to protect Buddhism.*

Nobody can witness that moment and do nothing. Monks, nuns and even secular persons dropped to the ground in reverence. People cried out for justice. Everybody kept looking into the flame. There was something more unseen there than they had ever seen. Something akin to divinity floated around that space and eventually floated throughout the world. Even though he wasn't there, Charles left something in Vietnam. He carried what remained to Grand Saline.

Immediately following the immolation, people all over the world reported having visions of Thich Quang Duc. Flames seem to draw them to deeper places of spirituality and justice. I would imagine that many people still have such visions. I know Charles did. I know I have.

After deep meditation, I journey to that intersection. Jesus shows me the way. In the distance, I see Duc. It is as if I know him. Regardless, I do know what's about to happen. The first couple of times I saw him, I tried to stop him. I don't do that anymore. I just want to be there with him. As he walks to the cushion, I walk too. Though I know where I am going, I'm always scared. Jesus is in me now . . . telling me that all is well. When the flames ignite, I can touch Duc. In that moment, something touches me like I have never felt. It is as if the Buddha and Jesus are one. Together, we are all burning for justice.

Through the Buddha that inspired Thich Quang Duc, Charles met Jesus . . . perhaps even for the first time. Slowly, he realized where Jesus was calling him to go. Like Duc, Charles knew that the elites would never understand his path. He knew that people would respond like South Vietnamese First Lady Madame Ngo Dinh Nhu did after Duc's immolation, "I clapped my hands at the sight of that monk barbecue show." Charles knew that Jesus endured the same thing on the cross. In time, he would be ready.

The images are simply unreal. Fire engulfed Thich Quang Duc until he collapsed in on his self. Through it all, Duc exhibits an otherworldly determination to do what he feels called to do. Jesus journeyed to the cross. Duc journeyed to the intersection. In addition to Charles, Christians throughout the United States couldn't look away. The flames called to them. Perhaps, they, like I, could feel the burn. The words of scripture kept ringing in their ears, "Greater love hath no man than this, that he might lay down his life for his friends . . ." The self-immolation taught all who encountered it that one can't love God and be unwilling to lay down their lives for others. For most Americans, the picture was a picture of something that happened far away . . . until it got much closer . . . and perhaps even more real for many . . . on March 16, 1965.

Cold. That's all that she could think about. The world was just so cold. She prayed that she would light a fire that would warm the world.

Thich Quang Duc lit a flame in Alice Herz. The picture would not let her go. For a considerable amount of time, Herz meditated on what to do. At 82, she was desperate to place her body into the fight for justice. Moving by cane, she prepared to follow the way of Duc. Meditating on the meaning of it all, Herz started slowly moving towards downtown.

Detroit, Michigan was about to see something as radical as it had ever seen. Alice Herz doused herself in gasoline. After a few more prayers, she slowly walked to the middle of the intersection. Declaring that she was protesting the war in Vietnam, she struck a match. Fire shot up her entire body. Quickly, skin started to drip to the ground. The fire eventually moved to her cane. Nobody could believe what was happening. People wanted to help . . . but there was little that could be done. Herz made her choice. After a few more breaths, Herz crossed over into the land where evil was no more. Herz wanted her death to mean something. There is absolutely no doubt that it did.

A burning elderly woman filled television screens. Christians couldn't turn their heads. There were no excuses this time. The immolation of Thich Quang Duc was often dismissed as being something other. Christians couldn't dismiss it as such this time. Alice Herz looked like their grandmother. The war was no longer just killing young soldiers . . . it was also killing the elderly too. Christians started to wake up to an even greater degree. After interacting with the news of Herz death, Dr. Martin Luther, Jr. even sought out more information on the meaning of these self-immolations. In time, King began to see Herz as a modern form of Christ . . . or someone who lives out the incarnation of Jesus in a very real way. The courage of Herz left no doubt that justice requires everything we can give.

In response to a letter of inquiry concerning self-immolation from Dr. Martin Luther King, Jr., internationally known Vietnamese Buddhist monk Thich Nhat Hanh responded thusly on 1 June 1965:

> *The self-burning of Vietnamese Buddhist monks is somehow difficult for the American conscience to understand. The American press speaks of suicide, but in the essence it is not . . . What the monks said in the letters they left before burning themselves is that this action is aimed to alarm and awaken the hearts of oppressors and call the world's attention to sufferings being endured by the Vietnamese people. To burn oneself is to say that their cause is of the utmost importance. There is nothing more painful than burning oneself. To say something in this manner is to say it with the utmost courage, frankness, determination, and sincerity . . .*
>
> *The monk who burns himself has lost neither courage nor hopes, nor does he desire non-existence, on the contrary, he believes that he is practicing the Buddhist doctrine of highest compassion by sacrificing himself in order to garner the attention of, and to seek help from, the people of the world . . .*
>
> *I can hardly bare the confrontation of superpowers occurring in my home. Thousands of Vietnamese peasants and children lose their lives everyday and our land is mercifully ravaged by a war that is already twenty years old. I am sure that you, Dr. King, as one who has engaged in*

one of the most difficult struggles for equality and human rights, understands and empathizes fully with the indescribable suffering of the Vietnamese people. The World's greatest humanists cannot remain silent on this issue. You yourself cannot remain silent any longer . . . In writing to you as a Buddhist, I profess my faith in the universal uniting principles of love and communion. We, like you, know the universe bends towards justice and, with or without your help, know our struggle will not be in vain . . .

King was forever changed. The spirit of Thich Quang Duc and Alice Herz would stay with him for the rest of his life. Indeed, their witness pushed King to go further than he ever imagined he could go. Slowly, Jesus was being put to the flame. God was no longer distant. God was a fire in souls. The flames grew higher and higher. Charles was deeply influenced by it all. The names, thoughts and images never left him. The flames never subsided.

There was a little girl there. Children were no longer shielded from the flames. Their parents wanted them to see. There was so much more than the shock and horror of it all. It just took the flames to discover what.

Deeply disturbed by news of atrocities coming out of Vietnam, Norman Morrison turned to the life and witness of Thich Quang Duc for understanding. He found more than that. In time, he discovered his destiny. In daily conversations with his wife, Morrison spoke of his yearning to do more. His faith compelled it. Throughout the night, Morrison would toss and turn in bed. Images of slaughtered Vietnamese children tortured him . . . the bullets . . . the blood . . . the bombs . . . the horror of it all. Eventually, Morrison couldn't take it any more. One morning he woke up and dedicated his body to those children. In a nation where injustice seemed to be so rarely noticed, he knew what he was going to have to do. By the time he cranked the car, there was no going back.

On the 2nd day of November 1965, Norman Morrison exited his car and picked up his young daughter Emily. Together, they walked across the Pentagon lawn and Morrison sat his daughter down directly under Secretary of Defense Robert McNamara's office. Morrison walked a considerable distance and turned around. McNamara happened to be in his window. Inspired by his faith in Jesus Christ, Morrison doused himself with kerosene and struck a match. Screaming out his love for his daughter and his opposition to the War in Vietnam, Morrison quickly perished. McNamara would later recall that this was the beginning of the end of the War for him. In the notes that he left behind, Morrison declared his desire to follow the selfless and courageous example of Thich Quang Duc. In a letter to his wife Anne, mailed right before his death, that arrived two days after his self-immolation, Norman Morrison explained as much:

> *Dearest Anne, Please don't condemn me . . . For weeks, even months, I have been praying to Christ only that I might be shown what I must do. Early this morning in my prayers with no warning I was shown, through images of burning monks and children, as clearly as I was once shown that Friday night in August 1955 that you would be my wife . . . At least I shall not plan to go without my child, as Abraham did. Know that I love thee but must act for the children in the Priest's village.*

Norman Charles left behind a similar note. In the midst of his research, I've long wondered if he read the final letters of those who had previously immolated. While it is impossible to know for sure, it sure seems like he read something about all of these folks. Similar to Charles, Roger LaPorte was fascinated by the unbelievably selfless sacrifices that all of these activists had made. The flames drew him in as well.

Protests against the War in Vietnam grew larger and larger. On the 8th of November 1965, The Catholic Worker Movement, led by Dorothy Day, held an anti-war protest in New York City to burn its member's draft cards as over 1,500 looked on in support. One of the participants that day felt like he got a message from God. Roger LaPorte had a pro-war activist get in his face with a sign that read, "Burn Yourself Not Your Draft Card." LaPorte accepted the request. Less than twenty-four hours later on the morning of November 9th, one week after Norman Morrison, Roger LaPorte walked up to the Dag Hammarskjold Library at the United Nations Headquarters, covered himself in gasoline, and, while in prayer, lit a match. In the midst of the flames, he cried out for justice. LaPorte didn't die immediately. On the way to the hospital, Roger LaPorte looked up to give his last words before slipping into a coma, "I am a Catholic Worker. I'm against this war and all others. I, like the monks in Vietnam, did this as a religious action." He died shortly thereafter. In his eulogy of LaPorte, Father Daniel Berrigan remarked: "This is no suicide . . . This is a sacrifice made so that others might live . . ." LaPorte was a martyr. Charles followed suit.

Inspired by the self-immolation of Thich Quang Duc . . . on the 10th of May 1970 . . . University of San Diego student George Winne Jr. went to the main plaza of the university and doused himself with gasoline and set himself on fire. Next to him, Winne had placed a sign that read, "In God's name, end this war!" Another student tried to save his life and did for a short time. While at the hospital, Winne uttered his last words, "I believe in God and the hereafter and I will see you there." I think Charles uttered something similar.

In the 1970s and 1980s, self-immolations seemed to slow down in the United States. Interestingly enough, this is about the same time that Charles' thoughts of self-immolation seemed to slow down as well. While I am sure that there are a variety of reasons for this phenomenon, the lack of major wars had to have played a part. In the early 1990s, that changed.

Desperate to make a difference, Gregory Levey began to gather newspapers. Many of them contained stories about the Gulf War that was raging in the Middle East. Unable to stomach not doing anything to stop such a senseless slaughter, Levey began to stuff those newspapers in his clothes and walk to Amherst Commons near his home in Massachusetts. Upon arrival, Levey poured paint thinner all over his body and knelt in prayer. Simultaneously, he struck a match. Once the fire burned out, the only thing that was left was a cardboard sign that said, "Peace." Like Levey, Charles was desperate to end the war as well. He too prayed on his knees.

At protest after protest against the War in Iraq, Malachi Ritscher gave everything he had. Everything he had seemed to make little difference. Ritscher was desperate to give more. Quietly, he conceived of a plan. On the 3rd of November 2006 during morning rush hour, Ritscher ventured to downtown Chicago and set himself aflame on the side of the Kennedy Expressway, the busiest highway in the city. In a suicide note published right before he self-immolated, Ritscher spoke of his desperation to end the War. There was little question that he was very angry. Charles seemed to have some of that too. I would imagine that it takes a little anger to go all the way.

Throughout his lifetime, Charles bore witness to numerous self-immolations. Though there are countless others, I chose to focus on this lineage because I believe this is his lineage. Charles had the spirituality of Duc. Charles had the determination of Herz. Charles prayed like Morrison. Charles was an activist like LaPorte. Charles demanded justice like Winne. Charles just wanted peace like Levey. Charles was angry like Ritscher. These stories put together . . . combined with countless others from around the world throughout history . . . were fuel to Charles' flame. These folks served as his mentors. You cannot understand Charles without understanding his lineage. He did not self-immolate in a historical vacuum. Charles was a part of a long movement of God . . . that begins in the burning passions of Jesus and burns still in those who place their bodies to the flame.

4 // THE LAST WORDS

My Life/Death Appeal to Southern Methodist University and Beyond

SIXTY YEARS AGO WHEN I first walked on to the campus of SMU (having transferred from Tyler Junior College and being from a poor family from a small town), and walked up the steps of Dallas Hall, I thought it was the most beautiful sight I had ever seen. Three years later (for the first time, I don't know why) I saw Perkins Chapel as I became a theology student, and consequently received (1956-59) the finest education available anywhere, in an atmosphere of revolutionary thinking and acting (Perkins was the first institution of higher learning in the South to accept African - American students (1952), under the leadership of Dean Merrimon Cuninggim).

Now, as I walk around the campus I am astounded by the magnificent buildings with the names of so many very wealthy people carved upon them, and wonder what is being taught or promoted; after all, SMU is owned by the United Methodist Church, whose Social Principles represent one of the most progressive and humanitarian documents to be found anywhere (except for the atrocious nonsense about homosexuality). The Social Principles advocate such things as universal health care paid for the government, tax structures which favor the less fortunate, freedom for women to choose what method of birth control they want including abortion, opposition to war (it is said to be "incompatible with Christian teaching"), environmental stewardship in the form of law, public education for all ages with financial support where needed, abolishment of the death penalty, etc. I wonder how what is being taught at SMU measures up against these and the other Principles.

There are three areas I wish to address, two to be supported and one to be opposed and changed.

The first is capital punishment. The Methodist Church was the first major religious institution in America to publicly oppose the death penalty; but in Texas, where United Methodism is so strong, over 500 executions have been carried out since 1982 (over 150 with the big support of George W. Bush, when he vas governor—the warrants are part of the archives in the Bush presidential Library, of which the university is so proud). Pretty much everybody agrees that, capital punishment does not deter homicide, that it is enormously more expensive than life-without-parole, that sentencing is racially biased against African-Americans, that almost all who are executed are poor and uneducated as well as sexually and physically abused, and that the main reason for killing prisoners is to satisfy the vengeance of victim's family members (but many executed prisoners have families, too—who only want them left alive, not released).

Nearly all developed nations in the world have long-since abolished the death penalty, but America (especially Texas—Dallas County now sends more people to death row than any other county) seems to relish it. What are professors, staff, students and alumni saying about this?

Secondly, the Social Principle which condemns homo-sexuality and criminalizes the blessing of same-sex unions (one of SMU's most distinguished former professors, and a person with many other honors, Rev. Bill McElvaney, is on trial for performing a same sex union and will probably lose his ministerial credentials permanently) needs to be changed. The Southwest Texas Conference UMC (of which I have been member for 54 years) persuaded the UMC to adopt the "the practice of homosexuality is incompatible with Christian teaching" language in 1972, after having expelled my friend and graduating classmate, Gene Leggett after he announced that he was gay, leaving him and his family destitute. It is time after more than four decades for this wrong to be set right: Gene's ministerial creden-tials should be posthumously restored, and he could be recognized as a distinguished alumnus by Perkins School of Theology for his bravery and persistence under severe ridicule and persecution.

Unfortunately SMU is considered one of the least friendly universities in the nation relative to LGBT persons. This is astounding, given the sophistication of its students and faculty, and in face of a genuine shift in attitude so that a great majority of Americans have no problem with same-sex unions and don't consider sexual orientation or gender identity to be a problem. I worked with LGBT persons for many years, and I saw how painful and degrading it is to be designated by the UMC (most major denominations have changed their stance) as sub-Christian and something less than human. SMU could certainly do more to protect its LGBT students and encourage their participation at every level.

The third, and probably most important, area of con-cern is that of economic justice, especially as it involves racial prejudice. Certainly SMU is one of the wealthiest universities in America and many of its patrons belong to the category of super-rich. The gap between such persons and ordinary Americans (especially African-Americans) is so huge that atrocious is hardly a strong enough word to describe it. Methodism has always had a bias toward poor people, and has worked for laws to protect them and change their situation.

Right now, remembering such evils as the murder of Cheney, Goodman and Schwerner in Philadelphia, Mississippi in 1964, who wanted to help African-Americans get the right to vote and better their situation, it is a good time to ask what universities like SMU are doing to train their students in the area of economic justice, especially where racism is involved. America (especially the South) has never really repented for the unspeakable evils of slavery and its aftermath. Affirmative action should be promoted in every way possible.

Well, these are some of the concerns of an almost eighty-year-old retired UMC clergy-person and SMU alumnus, who is well aware that without supreme sacrifice on his part, his words about them will not be noted in any way. It is unfortunate that our species requires innocent suffering and death to get very much attention. I would much prefer to go on living and enjoy my beloved wife and grandchildren and others, but I have come to believe that only my self-immolation will get the attention of anybody and perhaps inspire some to higher service. Dietrich Bonhoeffer talked about the necessary deed, "and the fact that when Christ calls a person he calls him or her to come and die," as he did so nobly; he did not advocate (so far as I know) what I have decided to do—but others have done this, when they saw no other way to have any significant effect.

I am deeply sorry to do this to the hurt of my family (who know nothing of my plans, of course), and to create such a horrendous scene on this beautiful campus, but I have intended only to hurt myself, and not to damage any more than necessary the beauty of SMU. I know that some will judge me insane and an attention-getter (but I will know nothing about that), and other accusations to discredit my attempt to stop the death penalty and persecution of LGBT persons, and to promote economic justice especially for African-Americans.

I have chosen to do this at SMU, because I love this school and know what great influence it could have, and the knowledge that such an act here, by a responsible person might be effective in moving those who care to do more about these issues. I am attempting also to atone for my own inaction.

Charles Moore

June 22, 2014
Biography

Charles Robert Moore was born on July 18, 1934 at the height of the Great Depression, on the outskirts of Grand Saline, Texas, in a farmhouse where his father was a sharecropper. He was educated in the town's public schools, was a Boy Scout (Order of the Arrow; Jamboree in Valley Forge 1950), attended Sunday School and was president of the Youth Fellowship at First Methodist Church, which recommended him for ministry in 1952 after graduation from high school, where he had been president of Student Council—and ranked second in his class. He graduated from Tyler Junior College (Highest Honors) in 1954, then earned a B.A. degree (Departmental Distinction) from Southern Methodist University in 1956 and a B.D. from Perkins School of Theology at SMU (High Honors) in 1959.

He served student pastorates in East Texas from 1953 to 1959, and was Associate Pastor at First Methodist in Carthage 1959-60, before transferring to the Southwest Texas Conference to Serve as Associate Pastor at Jefferson Methodist in San Antonio 1960-61, then appointed to St Matthew's Methodist in San Antonio, where he served for four years. He went in 1965 to do post-graduate studies at Boston and Harvard universities, while serving St. Stephen's Methodist in West Roxbury. One of his sermons was published by the Christian Century Pulpit magazine at that time.

He moved with his family to an inner city ghetto in Chicago where he and his wife worked as staff members of the Ecumenical Institute. They served two terms in India, one in a Bombay slum and the other in a small impoverished village. He was a master teacher leading seminars across North America and the head of several religious houses. Following a divorce from his wife of 25 years, he was assigned to Brussels and travelled throughout Western Europe as well as to Africa and the Middle East, promoting the Institute's development projects. He returned to serve the United Church in Woodsboro, Texas and the United Church of Christ in Lockhart, finishing his active ministry with a ten-year pastorate at Grace United Methodist Church in Austin, where he opened the 100-year-old congregation to homosexual persons, worked against the death penalty and served poor persons in the city. At the time of his retirement in 2000 he received awards from Parents & Friends of Lesbians and Gays (PFLAG) and the Texas Coalition to Abolish the Death Penalty.

For almost a decade, he and his wife, Barbara, have lived close to his grandchildren in Allen, Texas.

Finally

What I have decided to do today is not an impulsive act, since I have been wrestling for several years with a distinct calling to give my death on behalf of such concerns as I have already mentioned; by "calling" I mean the fact that the idea has come to me (and apparently to no one else, unless others in America have been seized by it and been unable to respond, as has been the case with me up to now): several scenarios have come and gone wherein my courage failed. It has been a long Gethsemane, and I'm ashamed of how distant and irritable I have been at times with my family and friends. Such plans cannot be shared with anyone lest they be implicated or at least responsible for not trying to stop a person from harming himself or herself. So there has been an excruciating loneliness about it.

While I was an active minister for almost half-a-century, I didn't risk much by taking a stand on controversial issues—although there were some moderate attempts. As a 19-year-old student pastor in East Texas beginning in the mid-1950's, I spoke in favor of racial integration and was cursed and evicted from parishioners' homes, and asked to leave another church for the same reason, especially after refusing to put on blackface and participate in what they called "the nigger minstrel," which the congregation expected their pastors to do. During the early 60's the congregation I served in San Antonio was the first to have a pulpit/choir exchange with an African American church, and we worked to integrate public facilities in the neighborhood. Later, in the late 60's and early 70's I lived, along with my family, in an African-American ghetto on the West Side of Chicago and participated in a community development project with the Ecumenical Institute: Chicago. We also went to India twice to serve in slums and villages.

During the last 10 years as an active minister, I served a 100-year-old United Methodist congregation in Austin, where we welcomed LGBT persons and elected them to the highest offices in the church. I went without food for two weeks in 1995 as an appeal to the Council of Bishops to call for removing the discriminatory language relative to homosexuals from the Book of Discipline, which they failed to do. This is especially painful to me since it was the Southwest Texas Conference UMC, in which I have been a clergy member for 53 years, that started the war against gays by expelling my classmate (SMU '59), Gene l,eggett in 1971 when he came out of the closet. The following year, the SWTC sent a delegation to the denomination's General Conference where one of them crafted the "incompatible with Christian teaching" words, which have been in the Book of Discipline ever since, with the subsequent ban on clergy performing ceremonies for same-sex couples (on penalty of losing their ministerial credentials). The SWTC has most recently refused even to interview a candidate for ministry who is purported to be lesbian but the Judicial Council (the denomination's supreme court) has over-ruled that action. While in Austin, I worked with the Texas Coalition to Abolish the Death Penalty, and stood vigil in front of George W. Bush's governor's mansion during more than 100 executions he approved.

I have not listed these efforts as a boast; I am not proud of the timidity they represent and their avoidance of physical danger.

What I am most ashamed of is that, since retirement in 2000, I have been completely inactive: having lived in arch-conservative places like Tyler and the Northern Suburbs of Dallas, I would not (as more than one pastor has assured me) be welcomed in any United Methodist Congregation. One of John Wesley's rules for Methodists (which is still supposed to be in effect) is the willingness to be "the filth and offscouring of the world"—that is, to be persecuted for speaking out against injustice (as he did, for example, against slavery). I have been nothing but a cringing coward . . . year after year for well over a decade . . . still, I do not see any significant way to influence important issues. Should I affiliate with a church and try through normal bureaucratic structures to affect policies toward a more just and merciful position? Or failing that, perhaps I could stand up during worship services and shout, like the prophets of old—maybe even get arrested. Would that lone wolf approach accomplish anything? Well, at least it should be attempted—but I find it impossible to do, because that is a matter of taking up one's cross daily (as Jesus said) and suffering the unrelenting attacks from those who just want to be left alone with their cruel prejudices—which also involves putting one's family in the middle of it, when they do not want to be there.

Is it more courageous, then, to burn oneself to death in a public place, suffering only for a few moments but attracting worldwide attention, as in the case of Buddhist monks in Vietnam, and the young man in Tunisia who started revolutions across the whole Middle East? It is heroic to face the flames, but then the consequences are left for everybody else to deal with. Long-term suffering for a cause (Mandela in prison for so many years, for example) is very admirable, still under torture, there is life, with the heart beating and lungs pumping air, and perhaps the hope of escape. But to bring everything to an end forever, and not to know what good (or evil) might come of it—that is a self-execution terrifying to contemplate. Giving up everything without knowing the result is ultimate unselfishness—and many have done it through the centuries, though mostly at the hands of someone else rather than one's own. Once the match is struck it is too late to reconsider. And what if the attempt is botched, and one is condemned to horrific suffering for a long time? Or perhaps the police discover the paraphernalia, and the potential self-immolater is hauled off to jail or a mental hospital.

Anyway, added to my consternation about what has happened to the State of Texas under governors George W. Bush and Rick Perry: over 400 executions, refusal to provide healthcare for so many thousands, brutal cuts in education funding, the law against same-sex couples (even the anti-sodomy rule is still on the books, after being declared unconstitutional by the U.S. Supreme Court), the attempt to outlaw all abortions, regardless of the situation, voter-registration rules aimed at excluding minorities—and then my alma mater, with the decisive promotion by the dean of Perkins Seminary, decided to incorporate the George W. Bush Presidential Center (including a policy institute) as part of the university; when the policies of the Bush administration are compared with the Social Principles of the United Methodist Church, almost all of them are in conflict (with the glaring exception of discrimination against people on the basis of sexual orientation, where there is complete agreement). No presidential library should be on a church university campus in the first place, but surely not a political policy agency, even if its positions were in agreement with the denomination. When I entered Perkins Seminary in 1956, it had become the first school of a major university in the South to bring about racial integration— and this was a decade-and-a-half before the denomination itself did away with racial segregation. I do not know of any initiatives now on the part of the seminary relative to justice issues, and it would be a very appropriate time to provide leadership relative to the treatment of LGBT persons.

So, my life has been, and is, a great misery over these issues, and I have done absolutely nothing about any of them for long time; I am a paralyzed soul, and cannot find rehabilitation: every avenue of effort seems closed to me, because I cannot or refuse to find a place to stand.

Yet there is one thing I have absolute control over: that is, the manner of my death. History will decide whether my offering is worthy.

It doesn't mater significantly who is doing the sacrificial deed today: what's important is that it is done by someone. However, it is critical that I, the one doing it, am a person in excellent mental and physical health married to a woman I adore and grandfather (late in life) to two delightful children ages 9 and 6. I have enough money to live a comfortable life in a delightful place on a corner with a park across the street. The turning leaves on the trees in my front yard are almost reason enough to keep on living.

I have traveled around the world three times and lived in great cities such as Boston, Chicago, Mumbai and Brussels, working with all kinds of people. It has been, with all its pains, a great life—especially for someone born and reared in the little town of Grand Saline, 60 miles east of Dallas (where, I am chagrined to say, racism still prevails and African-Americans are not welcome).

This is not an impulsive act that I am doing today: the calling to self-sacrifice has been with me since Sunday School and the crucifixion of Jesus has always been the most important thing about him to me (but, of course, he is one among millions of martyred women and men, who had the courage to suffer and die for the sake of justice and mercy). I have always felt that death for a cause was my destiny, but never so much as during the past several years—when it has admittedly been a preoccupation. It has been clear to me, too, that it would be self-immolation, since I am unable to get myself in a position for someone else to take my life.

I love everyday things so much: arising for a bowl of cereal every morning, greeting the sun through the windows, saying good morning to my wife, walking to the mailbox or driving down the street, reading a good book, throwing a football with my grandson or getting hug from my granddaughter, mowing the lawn and watching the azaleas bloom—the list is endless.

An Appeal To Power

I am a seventy-nine-year-old retired United Methodist Minister of 60 years experience, also having entered Southern Methodist University 60 years ago and earned degrees in English and theology. I have no significant achievements to offer from that period so that my influence on contemporary issues might have a significant impact—so I am laying down my life here today in order to call attention to issues of great human concern—especially homosexuality and the death penalty. When William Tyndale was burned at the stake in 1536 because he translated the Bible into language ordinary people could understand, his last words were, "O Lord, change the heart of the King of England"—and less than a year later there was a Bible in the vernacular in every church in the nation, and his translation became the basis of the King James Version.

There are two princes of the church for whose change of heart I pray today. The first is Dean William Lawrence of Perkins School of Theology at SMU; he is also president of the association of United Methodist seminaries and president of the Judicial Council, the denomination's supreme court; he was named "Notable United Methodist Newsmaker" for 2012 by the UM Reporter; he teaches church history and is considered an expert in United Methodism and American culture and United Methodist history and doctrine. Dean Lawrence was an effective lobbyist with the UM South Central Jurisdiction (which owns SMU) in gaining approval for the George W. Bush Presidential Center to be on the SMU campus.

The second is Bishop James Dorff, who supervises the Southwest Texas Conference UMC (of which I have been a member for 54 years), which is in process of uniting with the Rio Grande Conference, and will give Bishop Dorff enormous prestige for bringing about this union with Hispanics and he will have an unusual number of ministers and congregations under his care. Bishop Dorff was assistant to the bishop of the North Texas Conference for many years and has close ties to Dallas and SMU, currently a member of the university's Board of Trustees. It is to be assumed the Dean Lawrence and Bishop Dorff are close colleagues-

so, first I pray that Bishop Dorff will change his mind about the place of homosexuals (and other LGBT persons) in the UMC, and work to ameliorate the homophobia which was launched into the denomination by the very Conference over which he presides. My colleague and graduating classmate (Perkins 1959), excellent student and minister, Gene Leggett, was expelled from the SWTC in 1971 when he announced that he was gay, leaving him and his family destitute; although Gene was winsome and brave, there were no positions open to him. The following year (1972), a prominent lay member of the SWTC delegation to the General Conference, who was strongly anti-gay, crafted the infamous "the practice of homosexuality is incompatible with Christian teaching" words which were incorporated into the denomination's Social Principles. Subsequently, the General Conference criminalized

same-sex unions and decreed that any UM minister participating in same-sex ceremonies would be tried and expelled,
on a level with the most serious sexual misconduct offenses.
One of Methodism's very prominent personages, a member
of the North Texas Conference, who has been a professor at
Perkins, recognized as a distinguished alumnus, president
of Saint Paul School of Theology among a long list of other
notable achievements, is currently on trial for officiating at
a same-sex ceremony and will most likely be convicted and
have his credentials revoked.

At the June 2013 meeting of the SWTC, Bishop Dorff
sustained a decision of the Board of Ordained Ministry not
to interview a candidate who was said to be lesbian. The
Judicial Council (of which Dean Lawrence is president)
overruled him, and I do not know how the matter stands
at the moment.

The Southwest Conference has elected delegates to
the 2016 General Conference a year early, because of the
upcoming union with the Rio Grande Conference. I pray
that the Bishop's heart will be moved to work with the
delegation so that they could acknowledge that the expulsion of Gene Leggett was wrong as was the SWTC 1972
delegation's proposal to condemn homosexuality, which
was consequently adopted by other major denominations
(although most had recanted and fully accept LGBT persons). It would be a wondrous thing for the SWTC to lead
the denomination's repentance for this evil, and one day
restore Gene Leggett's ministerial credentials.

Secondly, I pray that Dean William Lawrence will do
more to move SMU, which is considered to be one of the
least friendly universities in America to LGBT students,
toward a more accepting attitude; sensitive as he is to
American culture, he is certainly aware that the nation is
moving toward a more sensible and human position relative

to sexual orientation. Also, as a church historian and leader of UM theological schools, the dean could encourage the great humanitarian document called the "Social Principles" be widely emphasized in seminaries and local churches. Most United Methodists are unaware that the Principles oppose the death penalty, declare war to be incompatible with Christian teaching, advocate for universal healthcare provided by the government when necessary, calls for rules to protect the environment, supports tax policies that benefit the financially less fortunate, insist on complete gender equality and a woman's right to choose methods of family planning including abortion, etc. The UM Social Principles (with the exception of the mean-spirited attitude toward same-sex relationships) represent a high degree of humanitarian concern, and need to be studied by those who care about social issues.

One good opportunity for Dean Lawrence would be to work with former President Bush. Sure the Dean knows that many of the policies Mr. Bush advocated, and still does, are in clear opposition to the Social Principles (such as war, tax structure, universal healthcare, capital punishment, etc.) Areas of benevolence such as funding for AIDS in Africa, support for women around the world, etc. that Mr. Bush has warmly supported need to be emphasized.

There is one particular principle, with which I am sure the Dean completely agrees, but that is opposed by President Bush, that is of supreme importance: opposition to the death penalty. Among the documents in the presidential library are the more than 150 death warrants enthusiastically signed by Mr. Bush when he was Governor of Texas (I stood vigil in front of the governor's mansion for more than 100 of them). Almost all developed countries have done away with the death penalty, but America (especially Texas, with over 500 executions since 1982) continues with it. Hardly anyone believes that it deters homicide, and it clearly does cost more than life without parole, it is racially discriminatory, and is used almost exclusively against those who are uneducated, poor and physically and sexually abused, plus the fact that trouble with drugs used to kill prisoners amounts to cruel and unusual punishment; the only reason for the death penalty is vengeance, which brings out the worst in its advocates.

So I pray there will be a change of heart that is needed in such great figures as Dean Lawrence and Bishop Dorff. I have confidence that others of lesser rank will also be moved to examine and perhaps change their attitude on issues of such profound importance to so many persons.

Finally, I would certainly have preferred to keep on living, to spend time with my beloved wife and my late-arrived grandchildren (Zachary age 9, the football hero in spite of Type 1 diabetes and Chloe age 6, the angelic personality).

This decision to sacrifice myself was not impulsive: I have struggled all my life (especially the last several years) with what it means to take Dietrich Bonhoeffer's insistence that Christ calls a person to come and die seriously. He was not advocating self-immolation, but others have found this to be a necessary deed, as I have myself for some time now: it has been a long Gethsemane, and excruciating to keep my plans from my wife and other members of our family.

My real spiritual life began 60 years ago when I first approached Dallas Hall at SMU. I always carried what I learned in those revolutionary years (1956-59) at Perkins School of Theology around the world wherever I served: this was always my soul's home, as it is this last day.

Charles Moore
June 16, 2014

Last Appeal

Although there are many other injustices about which I am concerned (such as racism especially for African-Americans, sexism in the form of males determining what women should do about pregnancy, economic imperialism which reserves wealth for a few and condemns everyone else to poverty, destruction of the environment for immediate need but killing the beautiful planet earth, the enforcement of inhumane rules of behavior on various categories of persons by religious groups claiming that God has told them to do so), but there are two specifically which have driven me to the radical act I am committing today: first, the death penalty, and secondly, the mistreatment of LGBT persons.

It is true that the number of persons executed around the world is small compared to other mistreated groups, but the finality of death makes the issue the most prominent of all; and the arrogance of a few who consider themselves good enough to take the life of a fellow human being who made a terrible mistake is untenable. The record shows that capital punishment does not deter homicide, that most persons executed are poor, uneducated and physically/sexually abused, that there is a racial bias relative to those chosen to be executed and that the methods of killing prisoners are cruel and unusual (even the lethal drug method). Worst of all, it is clear that the real reason for executions is hatred and vengeance, mostly to satisfy the families of murder victims (but the executed have families too—sometimes little children who have to say goodbye to their fathers and mothers).

Most developed countries have abolished the death penalty, but America (and especially Texas, which has executed more than 500 persons since 1982) continues with it. This practice is so abhorrent to me that I am willing

to undergo self-execution in a horrible way to call attention to it, and to plead with caring people to work for its
abolishment.

The second injustice which has driven me to this is
the persecution of lesbian, gay, transgendered and bi-sexual
persons: forbidden to marry, fired from jobs, ridiculed by
religion, etc. My graduating classmate and colleague, Gene
Leggett is a prime example: the Southwest Texas Conference
of the United Methodist Church (for which I have been a
clergy member for 54 years) was expelled in 1971 for being
gay, leaving him and his family destitute. The next year the
SWTC sent a delegation to General Conference UMC, a
member of which introduced the infamous "the practice
of homosexuality is incompatible with Christian teaching"
language; subsequently the General Conference criminalized homosexuality by making it an offense resulting in
expulsion for a UM clergyperson to participate in a same-
sex ceremony. Rev. Bill McElvaney, a very prominent North
Texas minister and former professor at Perkins School of
Theology, is currently on trial for officiating at a ceremony
and has lost his credentials.

I have worked closely with gay persons in the church
and have heard about the pain their rejection brings on
them and their families. It is past time for this to stop, and
I am willing to lay down my life to help bring this about.

I have chosen the campus of SMU to do this because
it could be so influential in bringing about change relative to these and other issues. Great persons like Perkins
Dean William Lawrence and other seminary teachers could
have great influence if they spoke out and led other faculty,
administrators and students to do the same. I have done
very little, but now I offer my all, in the presence of this
beautiful school which was the beginning of my real life 60
years ago.

SMU calls itself a place where world changers are shaped, and I hope that what I have done will contribute to that—in a more excellent way.

I was very disappointed yesterday that my courage failed and I did not carry out my plans on Juneteenth.

However, in the evening, there was a story on television about the three young men (Cheney, Goodman and Schwerner—one black and two white) who were murdered near Philadelphia, Mississippi 50 years ago today while they were a part of the Freedom Summer to help register African Americans to vote.

I should have been there, and later in the marches such as Selma—but I was afraid of losing my pulpit or my life. That fear has continued to dominate my life all these years, and I have done nothing to work against racism. So now, as I am almost 80 years old, and have little left to give, I offer my death to encourage others (especially now that voting rights are being taken away). It is enough that this deed on my part might help to keep the memory of those three brave men alive, especially in young people, so that they can work to rid America and the world of the scourge of discrimination.

Charles Moore
June 20, 2014

Another day gone by—another failure—but it is hard to face the flames. But I think today is the actual anniversary of those young men's murders. I would be so honored to be remembered with them.

CRM
June 21, 2014

O Grand Saline, Repent of Your Racism

I was born in Grand Saline, Texas almost 80 years ago. As I grew up, I heard the usual racial slurs, but they didn't mean much to me. I don't remember even meeting an African-American person until I began driving a bus to Tyler Junior College and made friends with the mechanic who cared for the vehicles: I teased him about his skin-color, and he became very angry with me; that is one way I learned about the pain of discrimination.

During my second year as a college student, I was serving a small church in the country near Tyler, when the United States Supreme Court declared racial discrimination in schools illegal in 1954; when I let it be known that I agreed with the Court's ruling, I was cursed and rejected. When word about that got back to First Methodist Church in Grand Saline (which had joyfully recommended me for ministry—the first ever from the congregation), I was condemned and called a Communist; during the 60 years since then, I have never once been invited to participate in any activity at First Methodist (except family funerals), let alone to speak from its pulpit.

When I was about 10-years-old, some friends and I were walking down the road toward the creek to catch some fish, when a man called "Uncle Billy" stopped us and called us into his house for a drink of water—but his real purpose was to cheerily tell us about helping to kill "niggers" and put their heads up on a pole. A section of Grand Saline was (maybe still is) called "pole town," where the heads were displayed. It was years later before I knew what the name meant.

During World War II, when many soldiers came through town on the train, the citizens demanded that the shades in the passenger cars be pulled down if there were

African-Americans aboard, so they wouldn't have to look at them.

The Ku Klux Klan was once very active in Grand Saline, and still probably has sympathizers in the town. Although it is illegal to discriminate against any race relative to housing, employment, etc., African-Americans who work in Grand Saline live elsewhere. It is sad to think that schools, churches, businesses, etc. have no racial diversity when it comes to blacks.

My sense is that most Grand Saline residents just don't want black people among them, and so African-Americans don't want to live there and face rejection. This is a shame that has bothered me wherever I went in the world, and did not want to be identified with the town written up in the newspaper in 1993, but I have never raised my voice or written a word to contest the situation. I have owned my old family home at 1212 N. Spring St. for the last 15 years, but have never discussed the issue with my tenants.

Since we are currently celebrating the 50th anniversary of Freedom Summer in 1964, when people started working in the South to attain the right to vote for African-Americans along with other concerns. This past weekend was the anniversary of the murder of three young men (Goodman, Schwerner and Cheney) in Philadelphia, Mississippi, which gave great impetus to the Civil Rights Movement—since this historic time is being remembered, I find myself very concerned about the rise of racism across the country at the present time. Efforts are being made in many places to make voting more difficult for some people, especially African-Americans. Much of the opposition to President Obama is simply because he is black.

I will soon be eighty years old, and my heart is broken over this. America (and Grand Saline prominently) has never really repented for the atrocities of slavery and its aftermath. What my hometown needs to do is open its heart and its doors to black people, as a sign of the rejection of past sins.

Many African Americans were lynched around here, probably some in Grand Saline: hanged, decapitated and burned, some while still alive. The vision of them haunts me greatly. So, at this late date, I have decided to join them by giving my body to be burned, with love in my heart not only for them but also for the perpetrators of such horror—but especially for the citizens of Grand Saline, many of whom have been very kind to me and others who may be moved to change the situation here.

Charles Moore
June 23, 2014

5 // INTERVIEW

Jeff Hood Interview,
Charles Moore Documentary,
"Man on Fire" (20 January 2018)

Interviewed by Producer Dr. James Sanchez.
*Slightly edited for clarity and brevity.

Dr. James Sanchez: So, who are you?

Dr. Jeff Hood: I'm a theologian and a writer and . . .
depending on who you ask . . . I guess
a couple of other things.

Sanchez: Your credentials are unreal?

Hood: Sure, sure, sure. Thank you. Under-
grad. Auburn. Masters/Grad. Southern
Baptist Theological Seminary. Em-
ory. University of Alabama. Creigh-
ton University. Doctorate from Brite
Divinity School at Texas Christian.

I've studied all over the world and found God in many strange places. In the midst of it all, I am most fascinated by the willingness of people of faith to put their bodies into the conversation.

Charles Moore is worth our study. Here is a man who committed an incredible sacrificial act with his fellow human beings in mind. I am interested in taking people into the flames. Fire purifies. Fire is not a negative thing. God uses fire to transform our world. So, did Charles transform anything? Did Charles transform himself? Did Charles transform our world? Did Charles transform those closest to him? Who did Charles touch and how had they touched him? Does the purification continue? It is our job to embrace these questions . . . not to run away from them and hide behind religion.

Sanchez: Purity through the flame. I love it. Fascinating. Tell me more.

Hood: You've got to believe that Jesus traveled through the fire. I mean, you know, from that Friday to Sunday. Think about the Garden. Jesus in total agony. That crucifixion wasn't no joke. Think about Charles experiencing all of the same steps that Jesus did before succumbing to the flames. You don't think Charles wanted to turn back? You don't think that Charles felt like God had left him? Jesus is burned. And so when we go to this place of thinking about fire, we've also got to see the, the metaphorical burning that happens on Friday to Jesus is the same burning that happened to Charles.

The Garden was on fire. Jesus was getting burned up. The disciples burned Jesus because they wouldn't stay awake. The society that Jesus came to save burned him because they continued to burn each other. And ultimately God burned Jesus because God turned his back on his very son. Jesus was on fire. Jesus knew things were getting worse. Jesus knew what was coming . . . he'd already felt the heat. This was a self-immolation and the self-immolation continues. As Jesus climbed up on that cross . . . Jesus was burned by God again. My God, my God, why has thou forsaken me? The crucifixion is a self-immolation. It's a burning. Jesus is giving himself to the flames so that others might live.

Something powerful happened on that cross. Something shook. Something quaked. The fire survived. The resurrection spreads the flames . . . bringing about resurrection within all who are willing to embrace the flame.

And so when we talk about fire, we have to talk about it in a way that speaks of liberation and sacrifice.

Charles Moore knew the Jesus that I am talking about. Hell, he lived it.

Sanchez: So you do see some, some direct parallels between Jesus and Charles?

Hood: No doubt. I'd question anyone's commitment to love that can't see the parallels. To second-guess Charles Moore it to miss the Jesus that was in Charles Moore

Sanchez: Strong words.

Hood: Well, people thought that Jesus was crazy as shit too. Crazy can make a big difference in this world Brother James. Hell, these guys make me want to be crazier.

Sanchez: Why was this flame special?

Hood: These types of immolations happen all over the world. In the flames, I always look for the presence of love. When I find it . . . those flames are always special. Make no mistake, Charles had the flames.

Think. Charles did this to combat racism. Most of the assholes I know won't even go to a meeting . . . read a damn book . . . give a shit at all about racism. Charles had so much love that he burned himself to death over it.

There was a fire in Charles Moore . . . and on the way to Grand Saline . . . nothing was going to put it out.

Everybody doesn't need to go out and burn themselves to death . . . but they do need to give their lives in the pursuit of justice/love. This is how you get saved.

Something happened to Charles. The fire of Jesus got hold of him and just wouldn't let go. Charles embraced it. Charles simply would not let go of Jesus. Charles was on the right path and we would be wise to jump on there with him.

Sanchez: So how did you hear about the immolation? Do you remember specifically?

Hood: I saw it online . . . in the Methodist Reporter to be exact. Initially, I wondered if he was nuts. The United Methodist Church seemed to have already come to that conclusion. After learning about Charles, God ushered me into a deeper place. Quickly, it became very apparent to me that Charles knew exactly what he was doing . . . in other words . . . Charles seemed to be the real deal. Charles was truly trying to follow Jesus. I believe he did.

People rush to dismiss Charles because to not dismiss him is to have to deal with what he did. He gave his life so that other people might have life. Which beckons the question . . . How far are you willing to go to follow Jesus?

For most followers of Jesus it's . . . not very far. Charles is one of the great martyrs of our time. Period. Nobody has to confirm that. His fruit speaks for it's self.

Sanchez: Tell me more about that.

Hood: I'm reminded of the rich young ruler. Our denominations/spiritual infrastructures are our rich young rulers. Jesus is saying, look here, you know, let me show you the pathway to justice. Let me show you the pathway to liberating the marginalized and the oppressed. And they see that the costs are too high. They just can't go that far. And so I think Charles, if he did anything, he showed what the cost of following Jesus is. Let's get real. If Charles had jumped in front of a child and took a bullet he would have been celebrated as a hero. In his attempt to die for all of us, he is treated as zero.

There is no question that Charles decided to give his life as a testament to what it looks like to fight injustice. You have to give

53

your body. You have to give your life. You have to give your soul. To do anything else is to be the rich young ruler and simply walk away.

But if you have the Spirit welling up within your soul, that quaking in your bones, that causes your feet to move for justice, that causes your mouth to speak for the oppressed. That causes you to never fear the flame.

For the follower of Jesus, fire should not be a difficult thing to talk about. We must never turn our head.

Sanchez: What made you go to Charles's funeral? What was it like?

Hood: The funeral was at a Presbyterian Church in Austin. I wouldn't have missed it. Even from the grave . . . or the funeral home . . . Charles continued to draw me in. Jesus was changing me. I could feel it. The impact was immediate and divine. I had to be there to say goodbye. Charles went the way of the Buddhist monks in South Vietnam. I believe they changed the world and Charles will too.

The monks were not alone. Remember Norman Morrison self-immolating just below Secretary of Defense Robert McNamara's window at the Pentagon during Vietnam? He changed the world. These moments of unbelievable sacrifice rattle the bones. I wouldn't have missed Charles' funeral. I think something in me would have died if I had.

While I expected him to be treated as a martyr and a saint, I knew that the people were too confused to do that. So, I felt like I needed to be there to be woke as to what had happened.

I will never forget being in that sanctuary and seeing the family. They just didn't understand. I wish I could have told them how I was experiencing it all . . . but I figured God would show them in time. Many of the gathered wanted to condemn Charles . . . but they quickly realized that they weren't going to get that from me.

One Methodist minister from Austin remains with me. He looked over at me and started describing Charles' immolation in a baseball metaphor, "Jeff, you get three strikes in life. Charles already had a couple of strikes going into this and by doing this he officially struck out."

I held my tongue. "Sir, you are a total asshole. I can't believe at a man's funeral . . . you would say such a thing."

I held my tongue. This interaction revealed to me as much as anything previously had . . . Christians in our day have no ability to understand what it means to give your life to Jesus. I mean, everybody wants to talk about sacrifice, but don't nobody wants to sacrifice a God damned thing. In the modern mind, safety beats out Jesus every single time.

Insurance. Alarms. Security. Plans. Directions. Policing .I was sitting there listening to all of these people who love safety and I was seeing up front what it looks like to live dangerously. I was seeing the cost of literally giving your life to Jesus so I could hear bullshit from these other folks all day long . . . all night long . . . the truth was laying up front.

Jesus was with him. What was left of Charles was louder than any of the bullshit chatter that was taking place at the back of the funeral.

Sanchez: You know? I think that's, that's really great. And we were talking about beforehand that we had spoken with some other ministers. The interviews weren't like this. What makes you different?

Hood: All of those cats are interested in doing something . . . I am interested in being something. I am interested in becoming more like Jesus in our world. Being like Jesus . . . not doing like Jesus.

These cats that you speak of . . . love to criticize . . . and don't know how to simply be. Hell . . . judging by the way they have treated Charles

. . . they'd have protested Jesus getting on the cross. They would protest Jesus. I mean, it doesn't get any bigger sacrifice than that. My God, they talk about Jesus holding the sins of the world and getting up on that cross and hanging out and they love talking about all the blood flowing down and on and on and on. Well, what's the difference between that and Charles giving his life, sacrificing his life? They both had a choice to make and they made it. I have a challenge. Those ministers need to get saved. I challenge them to hop out of their pulpit and actually join Jesus amongst the least of these. Give your life to the marginalized and the oppressed before you sit up there and talk shit. I don't have much patience for these folks. The shit they're spewing don't have anything to do with Jesus. "Get saved you evil fuckers!"

. . . and then your message will be worth a damn.

Sanchez: We share many emotions about this event. I was especially moved by your descriptions of going out there to the site of the immolation.

What compelled you to go? What was it like?

Hood: Visions of Charles filled my head . . . and I wanted to get closer . . . I wanted to commune with Charles. I wanted to commune with the Christ in Charles . . . and I did.

Honestly, I was scared. I was on a spiritual pilgrimage . . . and sometimes such journeys are difficult. Pulling through Grand Saline, I knew I was in enemy territory. It was dusk, late in the evening. Everybody looked pissed off. I didn't want to go any further down the old dirt road . . . but something was pulling me along. I tried not to think.

Closer and closer and closer . . . The churches didn't feel like churches to me. More like bastions of evil. I knew these folks weren't Charles' people. The community tried to ignore the entire thing. Charles' wouldn't let them though.

Bumper stickers and flags clearly illustrated that this was an intensely racist place. Then, I saw the parking lot. The people in the strip mall were already starring . . . in a deeply suspicious way.

Slowly, Charles seemed to alleviate my fears. I was mindful of the light . . . I didn't want to be in that shithole after dark. I can guarantee you of that shit. Danger. I guess there is nothing more dangerous than a self-immolation. Despite the distractions, my mind stayed with Charles.

Charles remained the whole time, I felt that the, the heat, I felt the flames and I felt the push to, to continue to give my life as a bodily sacrifice for those who are marginalized, those who are oppressed, those who are living on the edges, the least of these. And I thought about the flames and I prayed that God would, well the flames up inside of me, the same that Charles had. That I would walk the way of Jesus. And as I pictured the flames and was about to go, I found a red lighter on the ground. Regardless of where it is from, It has been a sacred object for me ever since.

The Spirit sets us free to see miracles in the mundane.

Sanchez: I grew up there. My family lives 10 miles east of Grand Saline. I've gone to that spot so many times. It changes me every single time and reminds me of how much I've changed. Change is good.

It used to be a hang out spot. It will never be a hang out spot for me again. A parking lot has become something so much more. It's symbolic to say the least.

Hood: Before Charles Moore, I'd never heard of Grand Saline in my life. I didn't even know it existed. But I've known many towns like it. Places that

God seems to have forgotten. Places stuck in the shackles of the past. Places of nothing. As a Southerner, I get it. Many of these towns seem to be the end of the line. For Charles Moore, Grand Saline certainly was.

United in history. United in destiny. There is only one way out. Death. In giving his life, Charles Moore sought to make a way out of no way for his hometown. There is no greater love. Greater Love Hath no man than this than he who would give his life for Grand Saline. Charles Moore is the great martyr of Grand Saline.

Sanchez: Can the town of Grand Saline repent of their racism? What would that look like?

Hood: It's simple. Tell the truth. Tell the truth about the past. Tell the truth about the present. Tell the truth about the future. It's simple. Tell the truth.

Hood: Grand Saline wants to rush past Charles Moore. Their Spirit is dead. Only the truth can bring about the resurrection that they so desperately need. They need to sit with Charles Moore and let him show the way. In fact, we all do.

This is one of the great spiritual

acts of our time. We would be wise to not let it pass us by.

Sanchez: So he lives?

Hood: Charles Moore will never die.

6 // END

WHAT DOES ONE THINK about the night before they die? Lying in bed, Charles Moore wrestled with the decision he had already made. Charles was desperate for his death to mean something. Tossing and turning, Charles clung to hope that it might. There seemed to be no other way. God was gone. Charles was left to walk this terror alone. The sheets seemed to be the only barrier between his skin and the flames. Just before sunrise, Charles heard a familiar voice. It was time.

Throughout the morning, Charles was tortured by what was to come. The only thing that kept him going was the promise of tomorrow. Saying goodbye to all that he loved, Charles cranked up the engine. The drive was overwhelming. Every intersection was an opportunity to end it all. Charles knew he had to die . . . but he just wanted to be spared the flame. It was too late now. God had already laid out the path. Though none go with him . . . Charles chose to follow. Looking at the gasoline and the matches, Charles knew it wouldn't be long. In the midst of it all, determination was his only solace. Unfortunately, there didn't seem to be enough of it. Charles turned the car off for the last time. In the midst of the familiar spaces, Charles started to utter his final prayers. The agony of it all turned moments into hours. After much time, he was ready.

Reaching into the backseat, Charles picked up the means of execution. Though the gasoline was heavy . . . it was nothing compared to the matches. Those little sticks of fire would end his life. Each one might as well have been a loaded gun. Charles slammed the door shut. This was it.

After some time, Charles lit the flame.

7 // LEGACY

David Buckel self-immolated on Saturday, April 14, 2018 around 6:30am at Prospect Park in New York City. I didn't know David Buckel. I only know his fire. That is enough.

Traveling throughout the land, David healed people. His medicine was fire. Repeatedly, David fought against evil to secure the rights of LGBT persons. His miracles often took place at weddings. That doesn't mean he stopped there. David spent the latter days of his ministry fighting to save the environment. On issue after issue and with person after person, David gave his life. There is no greater love than to give your life. David loved.

On the night before he was given unto death, David struggled with what he was about to do next. Can't breathe. Can't drink. Can't see. Can't hear. Can't feel. David knew that something drastic was necessary to wake people up.

The environment was imploding and people didn't care.

David grew more and more ready for what had to be done. Throughout his body, David could feel the anxiety. Wondering if there was any other way, he turned inward. After every possible thought, he knew what the answer was.

Observing the environment around him, David declared, "Into your hands I commend my Spirit." With that, he was on his way.

The sidewalk felt different tonight. It was as if his feet stuck with every step. The agony of picking each foot up was overwhelming. Yet, David continued. Something seemed to push him along. Unsure of what it was, David continued. Step. Step. Step. There were numerous times that David thought about laying down the supplies. Love is what held them up. Picking up his computer, David sent his final words to the world. It basically said, "May my love for our planet ignite in you a love for our planet." Not too much later, David arrived at the hill. It was time.

Kneeling, David poured a fossil fuel all over his body. After numerous thoughts about his love for all of us, David struck a match. Though the fire was immense, it was no match for the fire that burned within him. In those moments, David Buckel shared his love with the world. I can still see his flame.

"For David so loved the world that he gave his only life/love . . . so that whosoever believes in love will not perish but be one with justice forever."

God/Love occasionally incarnates amongst us. Such a phenomenon is called Christ. You will know it by its' love. Can't you see it?

The Burning Christ will never die.
Amen.

Thich Quang Duc.

Alice Herz.

Norman Morrison.

Roger LaPorte.

Gregory Levey.

Malachi Ritscher.

Charles Moore.

David Buckel.